GW00691718

MAKE SHIT HAPPEN

Quotes, Tips and Activities
for Inspiration and Motivation

Alex Martin

summersdale

MAKE (SH)IT HAPPEN

Text by Luke Forrester

An Hachette UK Company
www.hachette.co.uk

Summersdale Publishers Ltd
Part of Octopus Publishing Group Limited
Carmelite House
50 Victoria Embankment
LONDON
EC4Y 0DZ
UK

www.summersdale.com

Printed and bound in the Czech Republic

ISBN: 978-1-78685-562-6

Substantial discounts on bulk quantities of Summersdale books are available to corporations, professional associations and other organisations. For details contact general enquiries: telephone: +44 (0) 1243 771107 or email: enquiries@summersdale.com.

TO...............................

FROM...........................

Introduction

We all want to be successful at work or in our studies, in good physical shape, popular with our friends and confident in our abilities. But life can be overwhelming sometimes – where do you even start? How do you motivate yourself to keep going? With simple, bite-sized tips on positivity, motivation and perseverance, this collection of inspiring quotations and practical advice will help you unlock your potential, enabling you to deal with whatever challenges life throws at you on your way to the top. Covering all areas of life, from work to friendship to diet, this little book will leave you feeling inspired, empowered – and ready to make shit happen!

Set clear goals

Deciding you're going to get your life in order and realise your full potential is the beginning of your journey to be the best possible you, but unless you set clear, attainable goals you'll quickly lose motivation. Rather than vague generalisations, think about specific things you want to achieve, whether it's gaining a promotion at work, being able to run a 5K or making new friends. Knowing what you want is the first step on the road to achieving it.

Be sure what you
want and be sure
about yourself.

Write five clear goals here. Make them specific and attainable, and refer back to them often to see how many you have ticked off or how much progress you've made.

1.

2.

3.

4.

5.

YOU'VE GOT THIS!

Start by doing what's necessary; then do what's possible; and suddenly you are doing the impossible.

Anonymous

Visualise your goals

Paint a picture in your mind of what you want to achieve. Whether it's being in shape, securing a more fulfilling job or something specific like writing a book, visualisation allows us to experience our future successes, providing powerful motivation to achieve them. This isn't an excuse to daydream, however – you should also think about the processes you'll need to realise your goals. Having a clear mental image of where you want to be and the road you need to be on to get there can be a great help.

With our thoughts, we make the world.

BUDDHIST PROVERB

When you want something, all the universe conspires in helping you to achieve it.

Paulo Coelho

If one advances confidently in the direction of his dreams, and endeavours to live the life which he has imagined, he will meet with a success unexpected in common hours.

You're number one

The old adage is true: you can't please everyone all the time. We all want to be liked and accepted, but if trying to accommodate everyone else's demands is leaving you feeling stretched, just remember who comes first – YOU! Do what you need to do to ensure you have the energy and the motivation to tackle life head on – put your own needs and desires first, and don't feel guilty about saying no sometimes.

INVEST IN YOURSELF

Write a list of seven small things that make you happy. Each day of the week, treat yourself to something from your list, ticking them off as you go.

**Nothing will work
unless you do.**

Get out of your comfort zone

Sticking to what is familiar to us can be very comforting, but the really exciting stuff only happens when you have the courage to challenge yourself to do something outside of your comfort zone. Saying yes to things you wouldn't normally do is a great way to make new friends, gain new interests and learn new skills. If leaving your bubble seems daunting, start small: talk to a friendly-looking stranger on the bus, take a different route to work or try cooking something new for dinner. Don't be put off if things don't work out as you'd planned – it's not the results that are important so much as the change in attitude.

Make a list of activities designed to take you out of your comfort zone. Once you've done them, write how each made you feel. Did you feel inspired? Surprised? Refer to this list whenever you are worried about trying new things.

The replenishing thing that comes with a nap – you end up with two mornings in a day.

Pete Hamill

Take 40 winks

Studies have shown that napping can improve alertness, increase information retention and elevate mood. Twenty to 30 minutes should give you a boost while avoiding that groggy feeling when waking. And you'll be in good company – famous nappers include Thomas Edison, Albert Einstein and Winston Churchill, who once remarked, 'even if it only lasts twenty minutes, [a nap] is sufficient to renew all the vital forces.'

SEIZE
THE
DAY

The future depends on
what you do today.

DARE TO BE DIFFERENT AND ORIGINAL

Positive affirmation

Affirmations are a form of autosuggestion, which, when practised repeatedly, can break patterns of negative thoughts and actions. Scientists have claimed that using affirmations can actually strengthen the neural connections in our brains! Choose a handful of affirmations to focus on for a week or two. 'The world around me is full of love and happiness' and 'I am strong, capable and confident' are two examples. Repeat them out loud several times a day whenever you need a boost and you will be amazed at the results.

Write five affirmations here.
Repeat them to yourself
throughout the day.

1.

2.

3.

4.

5.

Just breathe and believe.

Jodi Livon

Words of wisdom

Inspirational quotes have an amazing ability to promote motivation and change the way we feel about ourselves. Best of all, you can always have them to hand when you need them! Write or print out some of your favourite inspirational quotes and keep them in places where you will see them every day, such as at your work desk or on your bathroom mirror. You could even pick a few from this book! Whenever your motivation starts to flag or you need a quick pep talk, simply recite a couple to yourself for a boost of positive energy.

The most effective way to do it, is to do it.

AMELIA EARHART

I GO WHEREVER
MY CREATIVITY
TAKES ME.

Lil Wayne

You have to be able to
love yourself because
that's when things
fall into place.

Learn to love yourself

Your relationship with yourself determines your happiness. Learn to treat yourself like someone worthy of love, respect and compassion, and your life will flow more effortlessly, abundantly and joyfully than you can imagine. Take a moment to congratulate yourself on your past achievements, think about some of the amazing things you've done in your life or appreciate your positive personality traits. Trust your intuition. The sooner you start treating yourself as the most awesome person you know, the sooner you will begin to realise your potential.

Fill this page with whatever comes to mind: doodles, thoughts, ideas, sketches. Let your creativity flow.

MAKE YOUR DREAMS A REALITY

Believe you can and you're halfway there.

Theodore Roosevelt

Turn off your screens!

These days it can seem impossible to escape technology. A typical day might see us staring at a computer screen at work, a television screen at home and a mobile phone screen all the hours in between. Reducing your reliance on tech can lead to better sleep, improved concentration and higher energy levels. There are some easy ways to cut down on screen time. Avoid using your phone for at least 3 hours before bedtime (try reading a book instead), leave the TV off when eating dinner, and take regular breaks from the computer at work. You should notice the positive changes in your energy levels and outlook within days.

Any excuse to get
away from the
computer screen
is welcome.

STEFAN SAGMEISTER

Motivation gets you going and habit gets you there.

ZIG ZIGLAR

NO TIME
LIKE THE
PRESENT

The most important meal of the day

Food is the fuel that powers your body. Our busy lives often prevent us from having a proper breakfast, but skipping this most important of meals can make you sluggish, tired and irritable. How are you going to be awesome all day if you haven't given yourself any fuel? Ideally, your breakfast will combine good carbs and fibre with some protein, so ditch the sugary cereals and instead try oatmeal with honey, fruit and Greek yoghurt, or almond butter on wholemeal bread. Either of these healthy combinations should keep you satisfied until lunch.

One cannot think
well, love well,
sleep well, if one
has not dined well.

Virginia Woolf

Is there something you've been wanting to do but haven't had the courage to begin? Write down the things you need to do to get started, and then think about how you might feel when you have achieved your goal.

A little help from my friends

Human beings do not thrive alone. A network of friends and family can provide support in times of difficulty, as well as helping us celebrate our successes. Surrounding yourself with supportive people will inspire you to be the best possible you! Friends provide perspective, ideas and suggestions, and offer help and encouragement in difficult times, so make sure you dedicate some quality time to those good people who are always there to cheer you on.

A friend is someone who makes it easy to believe in yourself.

HEIDI WILLS

Who do you consider to be your role models and heroes? What about them inspires you? Write down their names and qualities here.

The more I want
to get something
done, the less I
call it work.

Richard Bach

FORGE
AHEAD

One way to break up
any kind of tension is
good, deep breathing.

Deep breaths

The way you breathe affects your whole body. Slow, deep breathing tells your brain that everything is okay, and your brain in turn tells your body it can relax. By consciously adjusting our breathing, we can reproduce this state of relaxation when we need to de-stress. Keeping your back straight, draw slow, deep breaths through your nose, then slowly exhale through your mouth. Repeat for a minute or two and you will be left feeling calm and centred.

Don't count the days; make the days count.

MUHAMMAD ALI

All personal achievement starts in the mind of the individual.

W. Clement Stone

Create your own personal Hall of Fame listing your achievements. Big or small, if it's something you're proud of having done, write it down. Aim for at least ten items.

Clear the clutter

We all want to live less cluttered lives, but the process of physically de-cluttering our homes can seem overwhelming and we often don't know where to begin. Start small, clearing one room at a time. Clothes, kids' toys and kitchen appliances are common clutter offenders, but the good news is most charity shops would be glad to have these items, and you'll feel better knowing that someone else will make use of them. As well as the practical benefits of creating space and being able to find things more easily, de-cluttering will give you a psychological lift, removing stress and making you feel more motivated.

Get rid of clutter and you may just find it was blocking the door you've been looking for.

Katrina Mayer

Believe with all
of your heart that you
will do what you were
made to do.

ONE WAY TO GET
THE MOST OUT OF
LIFE IS TO LOOK
UPON IT AS AN
ADVENTURE.

William Feather

A good night's sleep

Sleep affects our overall health and well-being, our mood and our ability to focus and concentrate. It's very difficult to feel motivated if you aren't getting enough shut-eye. Sleep plays a critical role in immune function, metabolism, memory and learning, so having an early night will make you feel ready to take on the world the next morning. The National Sleep Foundation recommends we sleep for 7–9 hours a night. If you have trouble drifting off, avoid caffeinated drinks, watching television and using your phone for at least 3 hours before bedtime and enjoy relaxing activities to help you wind down instead, such as taking a long bath or reading a good book.

Tired minds don't plan well. Sleep first, plan later.

WALTER REISCH

List as many things as you can think of that your friends admire about you. This can be anything from kindness to punctuality – if you've been complimented on it, add it to the list.

Avoid social-media envy

Social-media envy is the feeling we get when we compare our own, ordinary lives with the seemingly perfect ones of people we see on social media. But remember that social media is a curated 'highlights' reel. No one advertises the mundane or unpleasant parts of their lives on social media, so all the showboating is giving you a misleading impression. Try to focus instead on the amazing things happening in *your* life, no matter how small, and in the world around you. It may not look perfect, but at least it's real.

A goal is a dream
with a deadline.

NAPOLEON HILL

It's not the mountain we conquer, but ourselves.

EDMUND HILLARY

Life isn't about waiting
for the storm to pass...
it's about learning to
dance in the rain.

IMPROVISE.
ADAPT.
OVERCOME.

Happiness is a journey, not a destination.

Anonymous

Think of a challenge you've overcome. What did you learn about yourself from that experience? Write about it on these pages.

Turn failure into success

Everybody makes mistakes or loses out sometimes. The most successful people aren't immune to failure – what sets them apart is how they react to it. Rather than dwell on setbacks, think about what they can teach you. What did you learn from your experience? What could you do better next time? Using setbacks to your advantage in this way helps you grow as a person and means you can bounce back stronger and better than ever!

Failure is only the opportunity to begin again more intelligently.

HENRY FORD

However bad life may seem, there is always something you can do, and succeed at.

NEVER GIVE UP

With confidence, you have won even before you have started.

Marcus Garvey

Strike a pose

Just as standing tall helps to make you feel more confident, holding a power pose can boost your levels of testosterone (associated with confidence) and reduce your levels of cortisol (associated with stress). A power pose involves spreading your body out to take up as much space as you can – chest wide, back straight, arms spread! The best-known and easiest power pose is nicknamed the 'Wonder Woman'. Simply stand tall with your chest out and your hands on your hips. If you're at work and feel a bit embarrassed about posing so publicly, don't fret: 2 minutes is all you need, so nip to the loo and work that pose!

Picture your perfect day.
Now draw your vision.
Which parts of your
drawing can you start
creating today?

You are never too old
to set another goal or
to dream a new dream.

The more we do, the more we can do.

William Hazlitt

Small steps

Thinking about what we want to achieve in life can often seem overwhelming. There's nothing wrong with dreaming big, but deciding how to tackle such gargantuan challenges can destroy motivation. The solution is to begin with small steps. If you plan on writing a novel, then start by thinking of potential storylines or set yourself a weekly target for a small, undaunting number of words. If you want to run a marathon, begin with a light jog around the block. Once you're in the habit of completing small, achievable targets, your grander dreams will come to fruition before you realise it!

A journey of a thousand miles begins with a single step.

LAO TZU

Follow your dreams. They know the way.

Kobi Yamada

You cannot
find peace by
avoiding life.

MICHAEL CUNNINGHAM

Create a routine

A morning routine provides a sense of structure and familiarity, which can be highly beneficial. Once you've established a routine, all the things which you would normally spend mental energy on thinking about – such as preparing breakfast, having a shower or getting the kids ready for school – become automatic, meaning you'll have greater reserves of will-power for the really important stuff. Research by the Heidelberg University of Education found that people tend to be most productive and proactive in the morning, so making best use of this time is vital.

Routine, in an
intelligent man, is a
sign of ambition.

W. G. AUDEN

Write out an invigorating and motivating 30-minute morning routine for yourself that gets all your most important morning activities done efficiently, leaving you ready to face the day.

....

....

....

....

....

....

....

....

EXPECT PROBLEMS
AND EAT THEM
FOR BREAKFAST.

Alfred A. Montapert

GET UP AND GET GOING

The power of exercise

It goes without saying that exercise is good for you. It lowers your stress levels, increases your life expectancy, lifts your mood and improves your sleep. It also goes without saying that most people find any excuse to AVOID exercising. If you're struggling with your motivation, here are some tricks to help fire your enthusiasm. Lay out your running kit or gym bag the night before (some people even wear theirs to bed!). Ask a friend to be a gym buddy to provide both company and support. Set yourself little challenges, such as running a certain distance, or swimming a number of laps. Once you're exercising regularly you'll feel more energetic and productive.

I exercise every day. It's what makes me happy.

Andie MacDowell

In what ways did you surprise yourself this week? Did you do something you never thought you'd be able to do? Write about it here.

There's nothing more intoxicating than doing big, bold things.

Jason Kilar

*Courage is found
in unlikely places.*

J. R. R. TOLKIEN

Life is what
you make it.

MARILYN MONROE

A positive workspace

We spend the bulk of our time at our jobs, but our workspaces are often sterile or just plain dull. Given that we often need to seek inspiration at work, why not create an environment designed to deliver just that? Framed photos of family and friends can remind us of the support we have and provide positive vibes; artwork can get our creative juices flowing; posters of motivational quotes by great thinkers can inspire us to power through adversity; plants can purify the air you're breathing, and have been shown to reduce blood pressure, mental fatigue and stress levels. With just a few small changes you can change your boring workspace in to a den of productivity!

A wise man will make
more opportunities
than he finds.

YOU CAN AND YOU WILL

Think about your bucket list
– a list of things you want
to do or see before you die.
Typically these are out-of-
the-ordinary activities, such
as skydiving, writing a novel
or climbing Kilimanjaro.
What would be on yours?

Don't worry

All of us worry from time to time, about our relationships, work, how others perceive us and whether we'll attain our goals, among other things. Though occasional worries are perfectly normal, worrying all the time can be unhealthy, sapping your energy and lowering your confidence levels. If you find yourself constantly anxious, bring your worries out into the light and really examine them. Is the problem you are obsessing over likely to actually happen? Is it really so bad? What could you do to prevent your worst fears from happening? If there's something you can do to address your worries, do them; if there's not, try to focus on something else – perhaps on one of your positive affirmations from pp.30–31.

Don't give in to your fears... if you do, you won't be able to talk to your heart.

Paulo Coelho

Doubt whom you will, but never yourself.

CHRISTIAN NESTELL BOVEE

Don't compare yourself to others

It is tempting to measure our achievements against those of others. The trouble is that there is always going to be someone who is smarter than us, richer than us, or in better shape than us. Instead of using other people as a yardstick for success, stay focused on YOU. Think about how much you've progressed recently and all the things you've achieved. Congratulate yourself on your growth and look forward to the challenges ahead. Life is not a competition and everyone is on their own journey – concentrate on your own progress, rather than everyone else's.

Write your own fairy tale. If you could create a 'happily ever after' story of your life, how would it go?

LEARN TO LAUGH IN THE FACE OF FEAR

You are not
stuck where you
are unless you
decide to be.

Wayne W. Dyer

Opportunities don't happen; you create them.

CHRIS GROSSER

Think of the benefits

We all have moments where our motivation flags and we ask ourselves, 'Why am I doing this?' Use these moments as opportunities to remind yourself of the benefits of your hard work. Try to think of the bigger picture and how good you will feel when you achieve your goals. If you are struggling to motivate yourself to go to the gym, for instance, then picture how much better you will feel when you're fitter and happier with your body; or if you have been putting off updating your CV, just imagine yourself securing a job in the career you want as a result of the effort you put into the perfect CV.

IF YOU WAIT,
ALL THAT HAPPENS
IS THAT YOU
GET OLDER.

Mario Andretti

The only way of discovering the limits of the possible is to venture a little way past them into the impossible.

The way to
get started is to
quit talking and
begin doing.

WALT DISNEY

Be mindful

Slowing down and reconnecting with your body can help you embrace the present moment and feel less stressed. Practising mindfulness is a great way to do this. As you go about your day, start focusing on your surroundings: what can you see, hear, smell and feel? When eating take note of the feel, flavours, smells and heat of the food, or, when showering, really focus on the comfort the warm water brings. On a clear day, head outside and really listen to the birds singing, feel the warmth of the sun on your face, smell the flowers in bloom. Mindfulness is as simple as giving activities your full attention rather than performing them mindlessly – existing 'in the moment'. Reconnecting with your body will help you really savour life and all it has to offer!

Make a list of activities where you tend to 'zone out', such as when you are eating or walking to work or the shops. In the future, try exercising mindfulness during these activities.

Always do what you are afraid to do.

Ralph Waldo Emerson

BE BIGGER,
BE BETTER,
BE BOLDER

Money is one of the prime sources of stress for many people, which means it's a great area in which to make real improvements to our lives. While not the most exciting of activities, sitting down to examine your income against your outgoings can help you get on top of your spending, providing some stress-busting financial de-cluttering and (hopefully) giving you some extra cash at the end of the month. Take a look at your most recent bank statement and see if there are any areas in which you could make some savings – daily coffees, meals out and redundant direct debits or insurance policies are common offenders. Gaining control of your finances will be a weight off your shoulders and leave you feeling energised and motivated.

Tell me, what is it you plan to do with your one wild and precious life?

Mary Oliver

Make a list of unnecessary
expenses you can cut
out of your budget.
How much do you think
you could save?

Instead of wondering when your next vacation is, maybe you ought to set up a life you don't need to escape from.

The 'if-then' plan

Putting things off is passing the buck to your future self. The trouble is that if you're lacking the willpower to do the things you find tedious or difficult now, you're also unlikely to have it later on. Making an 'if-then' plan can massively reduce the likelihood of procrastination. 'If-then' involves a hypothetical situation and the resulting action – so if X happens, then you will do Y. For example, your plan might stipulate that IF it is 3 p.m., THEN you will return those important calls; or IF it is Friday, THEN you will go to the gym before work. Studies have shown we respond well to these plans, as they dramatically reduce the demands placed on our willpower by ensuring we've made the right decision well ahead of the critical moment.

Make your own 'if-then' plans for all areas of your life – work, exercise, socialising. Aim for at least ten simple 'if-then' statements that will help simplify your decision-making.

Make voyages!
Attempt
them! There's
nothing else.

TENNESSEE WILLIAMS

If you can find a path with no obstacles, it probably doesn't lead anywhere.

Frank A. Clark

REMIND YOURSELF HOW MUCH THIS MEANS

Accept the
challenges so that
you may feel the
exhilaration
of victory.

GEORGE S. PATTON

You've got to seize
the opportunity if it is
presented to you.

Be open to opportunities

Opportunity knocks more often than we might think – the important thing is to recognise when it does. By being open to more experiences, even if we sometimes find them trying, we open ourselves up to opportunities. For example, going out to lunch with a work colleague might lead to the development of a new project; or going to a yoga class with a friend could be the beginning of an enjoyable new hobby. While it can be tempting to play it safe, the most successful people look for opportunity even in unlikely places and say yes to new experiences.

IF YOU LOVE WHAT YOU ARE DOING, YOU WILL BE SUCCESSFUL.

Albert Schweitzer

Discover your passion

Are you feeling stuck in a rut? Do you feel like quitting your job and following your dreams, but you aren't quite sure what those dreams are? There are a few ways to help discover your passion. Ask your friends what they think your skills are. Think about what you loved doing as a child – maybe you enjoyed being around animals, or spent a lot of time drawing. If money was no object, what activities would you try or how would you picture your days? Discovering our passions is the first step to a happier and more fulfilling life.

Write a list of things you love doing. Make it as broad as you like – from painting to horse riding, reading to telling jokes, playing basketball to watching TV. How can you incorporate more of these activities into your daily life?

You only get one
chance at life and
you have to grab
it boldly.

BEAR GRYLLS

A lot of people are afraid
to say what they want.
That's why they don't
get what they want.

THE
FUTURE IS
YOURS TO
CREATE

Your life is a book; make it a bestseller.

Shanon Grey

You are what you eat

What you eat can have a huge effect on how you feel. Foods containing lots of sugar, saturated fats and refined carbohydrates can make us feel sluggish and listless, so ditch the junk food and aim to eat lots of fruit (for antioxidants), fish (for omega-3) and wholegrains (for zinc). You'll notice a positive difference to your energy levels, your concentration and your mood within weeks. On a similar note, it is also advisable to reduce your alcohol consumption if you're a frequent drinker, as it is a depressant and can negatively impact sleep.

No disease that
can be treated
by diet should be
treated with any
other means.

Maimonides

Either you run the day or the day runs you.

JIM ROHN

IF YOU REALLY
WANT SOMETHING
YOU CAN FIGURE
OUT HOW TO MAKE
IT HAPPEN.

Cher

List three successful people
and write down some of their
attributes. What do they
have in common?

1.

2.

3.

A good balance

While putting in long hours to hit targets at work, finish that university project or get in shape for a half-marathon is admirable, it is important to strike a balance between our work, home and social lives. Spending too much time working can actually reduce our productivity, as well as negatively affecting our health and destroying our motivation. Taking some time out to relax, spending quality time with family and friends, getting enough sleep, exercising regularly and eating properly are all aspects of life that shouldn't be neglected – a well-rounded life is a happy one.

The secret of getting ahead is getting started.

One finds limits by pushing them.

Michael Posner

MAKE SHIT HAPPEN!

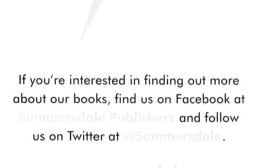

If you're interested in finding out more about our books, find us on Facebook at Summersdale Publishers and follow us on Twitter at @Summersdale.

www.summersdale.com